Swing and Strum

CONTENTS

A Fun Spot   page 4

Viv's Guitar   page 14

NATIONAL GEOGRAPHIC

Hampton-Brown

School Publishing

Blends with s

Look at each picture. Read the words.

Example:

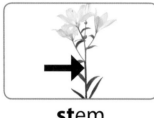

stem

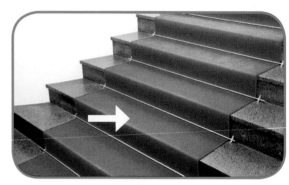

step

swim

stop

swing

spin

2

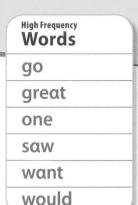

High Frequency
Words

| go |
| great |
| one |
| saw |
| want |
| would |

Key Words

Look at the picture.
Read the sentences.

A Big Swing

1. I **saw** a big swing.
2. I **want** **one** trip on it.
3. **Would** you **go** on that swing?
4. We **would** have **great** fun!

Is that swing fun?

Phonics Games
NGReach.com

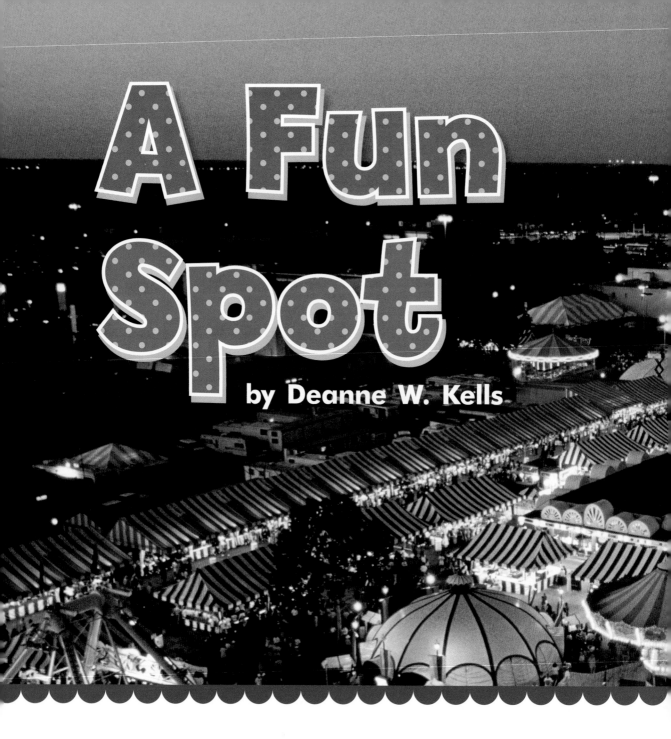

A Fun Spot

by Deanne W. Kells

Would you like to go to the fair?

The fair is a great spot.

You can have lots and lots of
fun there.

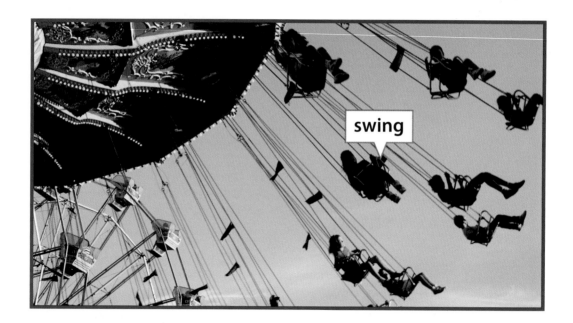

You can swing and spin.

You can win a dog. We saw a
big one!

hot dog

You can eat lots of fun snacks. Would you want to eat a hot dog on a stick?

You can see hens and hogs. A hog
is a pig. What a smell!

Would you go to the fair? Step up
to get a ticket! ❖

Blends with <u>s</u>

Read these words.

spin	swing	smell	snack
sit	stop	skip	win

Find the words with **s** blends.
Use letters to build them.

Talk Together

Choose words from the box
above to tell your partner
what you can do at the fair.

You can <u>sit</u>
and <u>snack</u>.

11

Triple Blends

Look at each picture. Read the words.

Example:

scrub

strip

string

strap

strum

High Frequency Words
go
great
one
saw
want
would

Key Words

Read the sentences. Match each sentence to one of the pictures.

1.

2.

Strum and Sing

1. What a **great** song! She can sing.
2. I **want** to sing a new song.
3. But I **saw** a string **go** pop!
4. **Would** she strum a song with **one** less string?

Will she fix the string?

Phonics Games
NGReach.com

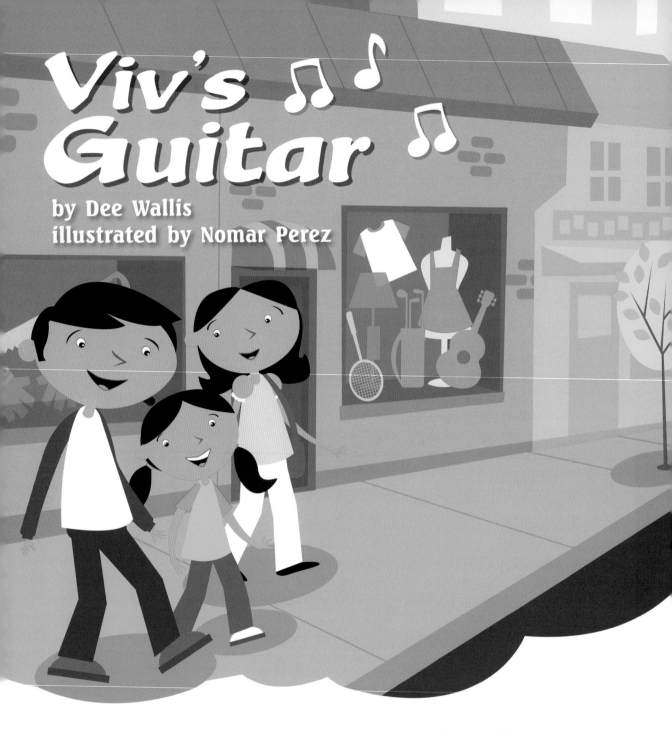

Viv's Guitar

by Dee Wallis
illustrated by Nomar Perez

It is spring. Viv, Mom, and Dad go out.

Viv sees a great guitar.

 I saw a great guitar. Can I get it?

I want to strum and sing!

How would you strum it? It has no strings or strap.

 See? The strings have sprung.

The strap is missing.

 I can fix it! I will bring it there.

Viv gets the guitar strung. Viv
gets one strap.

Viv starts to strum and sing. Mom
and Dad like singing, too! ❖

Triple Blends

Read these words.

strap	strip	hat	string
bag	strung	scrub	spring

Find the words with triple blends. Use letters to build them.

s p r i n g

Talk Together

Choose words from the box above to tell your partner more about the picture.

Her hat has a red spring.

Fun Spots

Look at the picture with a partner. Take turns reading the clues. Find the spots the clues describe.

- Go there if you want to swim.

- You would want to swing there.

- You can see lots of string there.

- She stops and strums there.

- A strip of grass is there.

- One dog is smelling a bug there.

Acknowledgments

Grateful acknowledgment is given to the authors, artists, photographers, museums, publishers, and agents for permission to reprint copyrighted material. Every effort has been made to secure the appropriate permission. If any omissions have been made or if corrections are required, please contact the Publisher.

Photographic Credits

CVR (bl) Daniel Martinez/Somos Images/Corbis. (tr) Syracuse Newspapers/L. Long/The Image Works, Inc. **2** (bl) Lee Pettet/iStockphoto. (br) Todd Warnock/Getty Images. (cl) David Crowther/iStockphoto. (cr) mikadx/iStockphoto. (tl) igor terekhov/iStockphoto. (tr) xyno/iStockphoto. **3** (b) Liz Garza Williams/Hampton-Brown/National Geographic School Publishing. (t) Juha Huiskonen/iStockphoto. **4-5** Robert E Daemmrich/Getty Images. **6** (b) Randy Faris/Corbis. (t) Doug Wilson/Corbis. **7** Gabe Palmer/Alamy Images. **8** (b) SweetyMommy/iStockphoto. (t) Alan Marsh/age fotostock. **9** (b) Scott Leigh/iStockphoto. (t) Jacksonville Journal-Courier/Clayton Stalter/The Image Works, Inc.. **10** Frances Roberts/Alamy Images. **11** (t) Liz Garza Williams/Hampton-Brown/National Geographic School Publishing. **12** (b) Michael Winokur Photography/Getty Images. (tl) Renee Comet/Getty Images. (tr) Mark Thiessen/Hampton-Brown/National Geographic School Publishing. **13** (b) Liz Garza Williams/Hampton-Brown/National Geographic School Publishing. (l) David Oxberry/Getty Images. (r) Ben Hamatake. **21** (t) Liz Garza Williams/Hampton-Brown/National Geographic School Publishing.

Illustrator Credits
11, 21, 22-23 Jannie Ho; **14-20** Nomar Perez

The National Geographic Society
John M. Fahey, Jr., President & Chief Executive Officer
Gilbert M. Grosvenor, Chairman of the Board

National Geographic School Publishing
Hampton-Brown
www.NGSP.com

Printed in the USA.
Quad Graphics, Leominster, MA

ISBN:978-0-7362-8030-3

18 19
10 9 8 7